A Guide to Identifying
Deadly Herbs

Written and Illustrated by
Julie Gomez

ISBN 0-88839-397-0

Cataloging in Publication Data
Gomez, Julie, 1964–
    A guide to deadly herbs

    ISBN 0-88839-397-0

    1. Poisonous plants—Identification.   2. Herbs—
Identification.   I. Title
QK100.A1G65 1997   581.6'59   C97-910100-X

Printed in Hong Kong—Colorcraft

Production: Myron Shutty and Nancy Miller

Published simultaneously in Canada and the United States by

HANCOCK HOUSE PUBLISHERS LTD.
19313 Zero Avenue, Surrey, BC V4P 1M7
(604) 538-1114   Fax (604) 538-2262

HANCOCK HOUSE PUBLISHERS
1431 Harrison Avenue, Blaine, WA 98230-5005
(604) 538-1114   Fax (604) 538-2262

Contents

Glossary

Annuals:
plants that complete their life cycle in one year: growing from seed, flower, set seed and die.

Anther:
the portion of the stamen that holds the pollen.

Axil:
the V-shaped angle between the stalk and the stem where they join.

Biennials:
plants that complete their life cycle in two years: developing leaves in their first year, producing stalk, flowers, set seed and dying the second year.

Bract:
a small, modified leaf near the flower.

Bulb:
a plant's underground, food-storage organ that has scales and fibrous roots at its base.

Calyx:
fused or open sepals that support the flower.

Corm:
a thick, vertical, underground stem that is bulb-like, but without scales.

Deciduous:
a plant that sheds its leaves.

Decoction:
boiling a hard plant material (such as the root).

Disk:
the flat compact area in the center of a daisylike flower.

Diuretic:
an agent that increases the flow of urine.

Expectorant:
an agent that stimulates the release of mucus from the lungs and bronchial passages.

Infusion:
pouring boiled or cold water over fresh or dried plant material.

Margin:
leaf edge.

Nodes:
swollen joints on the stalk where shoots, buds and leaves form. (Roots usually form at the nodes on creeping stalks.)

Naturalized:	a nonnative (introduced) plant species that is able to grow and spread, and behaves like a native species without human interference.
Panicle:	a group of flowers that bloom from the bottom up.
Perennial:	a plant that lives for more than two years.
Poultice:	an external application of plant material that is applied to a portion of the body.
Rootstock:	a spreading, horizontal, underground stem (rhizome) that sends up nods, buds or scalelike leaves.
Sepals:	the (typically) green petals of the calyx that enclose the developing flower and that support the opened flower.
Spur:	a hollow extension on a flower petal or sepal.
Stamen:	the organ of a flower in which the pollen is held.
Taproot:	a long or short vertical root.
Tincture:	the soaking of plant material in alcohol and water.
Tuber:	a swollen underground root or stem that produces buds.
Umbel:	a flat-topped grouping of stemmed flowers that resemble an open umbrella.
Vermifuge:	a remedy that kills intestinal worms.

Introduction

Although wild herbs are present year-round, they often go unnoticed until the arrival of spring. It is then that they catch our attention by showing off their conspicuous flowers that present a blend of sweet (and not so sweet) fragrances.

Many wild herbs (as well as cultivated varieties) have unique properties that are useful as food and medicine. While the majority are completely harmless, there are those that exist as a wolf in sheep's clothing. Numerous reports of accidental poisonings occur each year among inexperienced, or careless foragers that mistake a toxic species for a harmless one. Most reported cases involve young children. Herbs that produce noticeable seeds and berries are especially tempting, since children often like to sample their surroundings with their mouths.

Livestock, as well as domestic pets are not immune, and fatalities are not uncommon. Livestock are most vulnerable during the spring when they are put into fresh pastures to graze. Domestic pets (particularly cats) are poisoned each year by various garden and household plants.

While writing this, my dog chewed four leaves off one of my house plants (which he has never done before) and managed to swallow a couple of pieces before I could reach him. I quickly pulled the remainder of one leaf from his mouth, and picked the other three off the floor. (He knew I was working on this book, and I hate it when he tries to prove me right.) The plant which he ate is a croton (*Codiaeum vanegatum*) and is poisonous. Its seeds, leaves and stems all contain a toxic oil that can irritate the skin and be fatal if ingested. I quickly called my veterinarian and she advised me to withhold his food, offer him plenty of water, and watch for the following symptoms: vomiting, diarrhea, listlessness and muscle tremors. My dog did manage to vomit and showed no other symptoms—he was lucky.

Some wild herbs, while not lethal, yield certain properties that can cause dermatitis when handled, extreme discomfort if ingested or both. One of the problems that these deadly herbs present (aside from the fact that they can kill you) is that they often resemble harmless look-alikes, take for instance the lovely blue monkshood (*Aconitum columbianum*). Its attractive foliage and lavender blue flowers that resemble miniature bonnets clearly identify this species; however, fatalities have occurred for those who mistakenly ate its fleshy tubers thinking they were consuming wild horseradish (*Armoracea lapathifolia*). The poison hemlock (*Conium maculatum*) is another imposter. Its lacy foliage and intricate white flowers are deceiving, and people have died after eating the herb thinking they were consuming the harmless Queen Anne's lace (*Daucus carota*) that often grows in its vicinity.

There are more than 500 species of poisonous plants growing in North America, all of which possess various toxic levels and symptoms, depending on the species. This book discusses twenty eight of some of the most deadly herbs (wild and cultivated, native and alien) that can be found throughout North America.

Most of the herbs discussed have a history of medicinal use, and while this makes for fascinating reading, under no circumstance should these uses ever be practiced. All of the herbs discussed in this book are considered extremely dangerous. It is not my intention to discourage those who enjoy in the partaking of wild herbs (since I also indulge in such pleasures) but instead to reveal to you the potential dangers that often grow and blossom among our gardens and beyond. These herbs are deadly, but they are also very beautiful; each one unique, each one a treasure.

In case of poisoning contact your nearest poison control center immediately!

No book can be accomplished alone, and I would like to thank all those who graciously gave their encouragement, support and advice. The staff of the Oregon, Seattle and British Columbia Poison Control Centers, were wonderful in answering my many questions. Krista Thie, editor of *Herbs Northwest*, supplied me with information during the course of my research. My family, who believed in this project from the beginning, gave me wonderful support. Most of all, I thank my husband Christopher who has encouraged me from the start—he's always there. Finally, praise with a pat on the head goes to my dog Murphy, who unintentionally contributed his fair share to the introduction of this book.

Coyote Tobacco
Nicotiana attenuata

Flowers: white.

In bloom: May–November.

Life cycle: annual.

Size: one to six feet tall.

A foul-scented, sticky-haired herb with lower leaves that are long and ovate, and upper leaves that are short and linear. Leaves have long, hairy stems and alternate on a slender, hairy stalk. Flowers bloom in loose clusters on divided stems. They are long, slender trumpets that produce five small, star-shaped petals that are supported by a hairy calyx. Seedpods are two-chambered and contain numerous seeds. The taproot is long and branching.

Habitat: sandy soils, stream banks.

Poisonous parts: all parts; especially leaves, flowers.

Symptoms: handling can cause toxic symptoms. Ingesting causes nausea, abdominal cramps, vomiting, diarrhea, spasms, rapid pulse, weakness, blindness, death.

Notes: *Nicotiana attenuata* is a lovely herb to gaze upon when in bloom, despite its unpleasant smell and toxic nature. The entire herb contains nicotine which can be quickly absorbed into the bloodstream, so handling is not recommended. Eating the smallest amount is lethal, and fatalities have occurred when its leaves were eaten as salad greens. Livestock have died after grazing on the foliage.

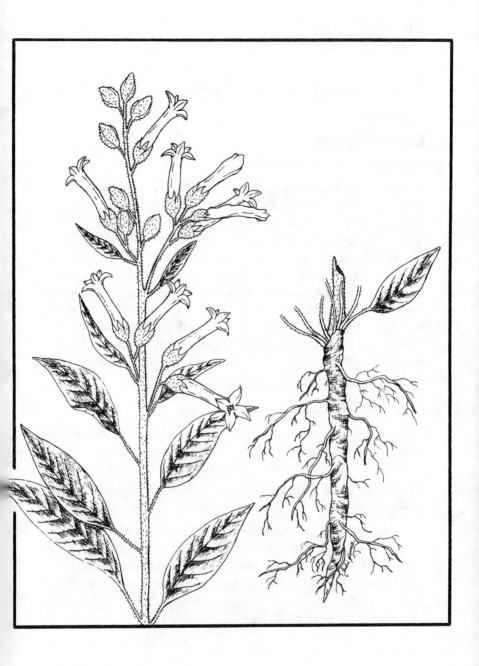

Death Camas
Zigadenus venenosus

Flowers: white (sometimes pale yellow).

In bloom: March–June.

Life cycle: perennial.

Size: four inches to two feet tall.

A slender, foul-scented herb with alternating leaves that become smaller as they proceed up the stalk. Basal leaves are long, slender and grasslike, and often exceed above the flowers. The stalk is smooth and nonbranching. Flowers bloom profusely in loose or compact clusters. They are star-shaped with three petals, three sepals and long upturned stamens that exceed them. At the base of each flower petal is an inconspicuous, tiny green gland. Seedpods have three divisions and contain a pair of brown seeds. The bulb is dark brown and has an outer scaly coating that closely resembles an onion, but lacks the onion scent.

Habitat: fields, meadows, pastures, roadsides.

Poisonous parts: all parts.

Symptoms: burning in the mouth, headache, dizziness, nausea, vomiting, abdominal pain, loss of muscle control, trembling, low body temperature, respiratory failure, coma, death.

Medicinal uses: bulb poultice for boils, bruises, swellings, rheumatism.

Notes: *Zigadenus venenosus* resembles the bulbs of wild hyacinth, common camas and wild onion. Human fatalities have occurred. Livestock (particularly sheep) are extremely vulnerable and favor the grasslike foliage and blossoms; the end result is lethal. So toxic is this herb, insects tending the flowers can literally drop over dead while sipping the nectar.

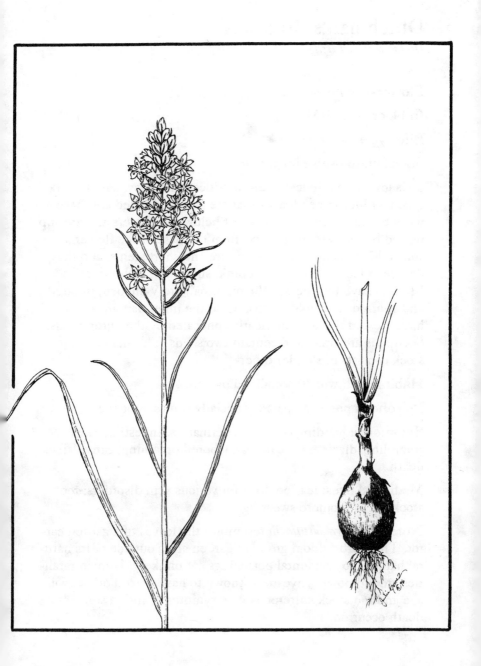

Dutchman's Breeches
Dicentra cucullaria

Flowers: white (sometimes pink).

In bloom: April–May.

Life cycle: perennial.

Size: four to twelve inches tall.

This lovely and delicate herb produces thin, lacy, pale to dark green, or blue-green leaves that are greatly divided and have a waxy texture. Leaves appear just below the flowers and are supported by long stems that rise from the base of the flower stalks. Flowers have a waxy texture and short stems, and they dangle in loose clusters from pink, succulent, arching stalks. Flowers have four petals, the outer pair are V-shaped, inflated and spurred with golden tips, while the inner pair are small, have crested tips and are nearly concealed by the outer petals. Seedpods are small and contain two seeds. The shallow rootstock consists of slender tubers.

Habitat: rich woods, woodland pastures.

Poisonous parts: all parts; especially leaves, rootstock.

Symptoms: handing can cause dermatitis. Ingesting causes trembling, dizziness, weakness, labored breathing, convulsions, death.

Medicinal uses: leaf poultice for various skin disorders; rootstock tea to promote sweating.

Notes: *Dicentra cucullaria* resembles the leaves of a garden carrot. This herb seldom grows in garden areas outside of its natural habitat, so accidental poisonings are unlikely. Human fatalities are unknown. Livestock known to have grazed on the foliage and rootstock suffered severe symptoms, and in some cases death occurred.

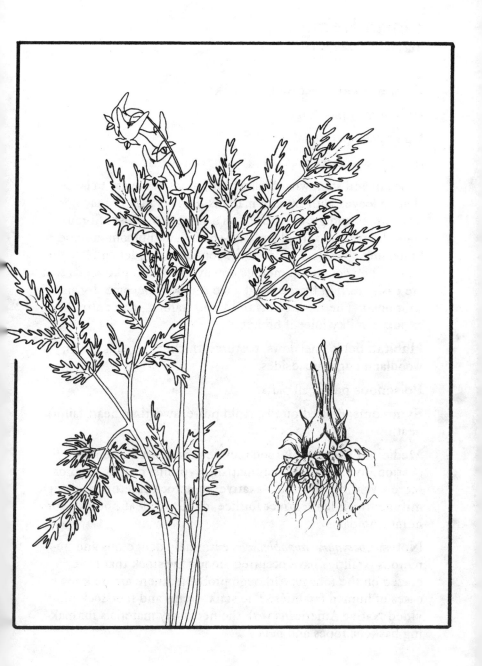

Indian Hemp
Apocynum cannabinum

Flowers: white (occasionally pink).

In bloom: June–August.

Life cycle: perennial.

Size: one to three feet tall.

This tall and somewhat bushy herb, produces ovate to lance-shaped leaves with smooth margins. Leaves may or may not have stems and grow opposite on a smooth, reddish, fibrous stalk. Flowers are small and bell-shaped, and bloom in loose, branching clusters. Seedpods are long and slender and hang in pairs. They contain numerous downy, parachutelike seeds that are easily carried by the wind once the pods become dry and split open. The rootstock is thick and trailing. The entire herb exudes a milky juice if broken.

Habitat: fields, meadows, pastures, thickets, stream banks, woodland edges, roadsides.

Poisonous parts: all parts.

Symptoms: dilated pupils, rapid pulse, sweating, heart failure, death.

Medicinal uses: weak rootstock tea for heart ailments, indigestion, liver disease, rheumatism, syphilis, dropsy, to promote sweating, diuretic, laxative; rootstock tincture as a vermifuge; fresh leaf extract for lice, dandruff; leaf poultice for hemorrhoids.

Notes: *Apocynum cannabinum* is extremely dangerous and numerous fatalities have occurred among livestock that have grazed on the foliage. Although probable, there are no known cases of human fatalities. The stalk, stems and rootstock provided Native Americans with the necessary materials for making baskets, ropes and nets.

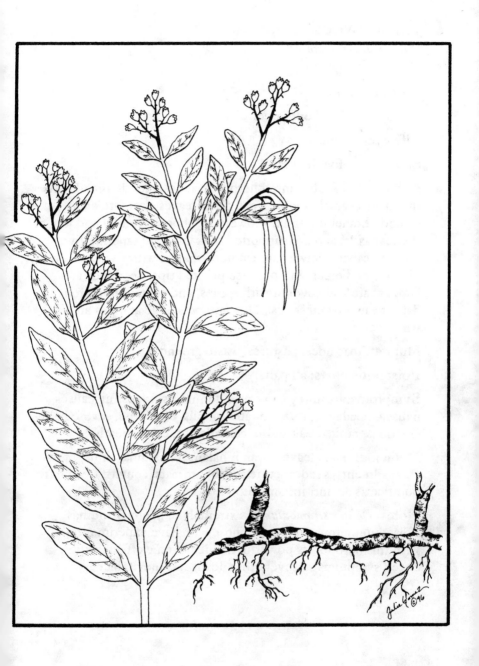

Jimsonweed
Datura stramonium

Flowers: white.

In bloom: May–September.

Life cycle: annual.

Size: two to five feet tall.

A showy, but foul-scented herb with long, smooth, broad leaves that have coarsely toothed margins. Leaves alternate on a smooth, branching stalk. Flowers are short-stemmed and join at the leaf axils, and are supported by a long and tapering five-pointed calyx. Flowers are trumpet-shaped with five petals that are long and erect, and produce pointed tips. Seedpods are large, ovate and covered with spines, and contain numerous dark, bean-shaped seeds. The taproot is large and has an off-white color.

Habitat: roadsides, pastures, waste ground.

Poisonous parts: all parts.

Symptoms: handling can cause dermatitis. Ingesting causes nausea, headache, thirst, dilated pupils, blindness, severe hallucinations, rapid-weak pulse, convulsions, coma, death.

Medicinal uses: leaves as an inhalant for asthma, sinus, bronchial ailments; seed tincture for sore throats, coughs; fresh herb poultice as an anti-inflammatory.

Notes: *Datura stramonium* is extremely dangerous and has caused numerous fatalities. Those who have experimented with this herb for its powerful hallucinogenic effects experienced symptoms so severe that death was inevitable.

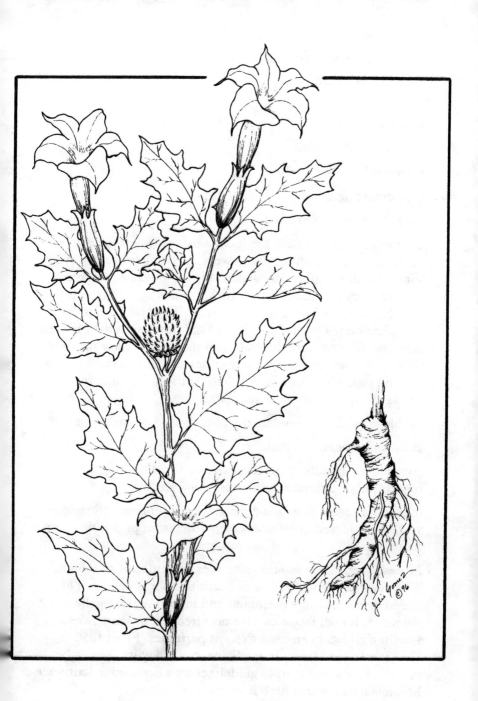

Lily of the Valley
Convallaria majalis

Flowers: white.

In bloom: May–June.

Berries: July–September.

Life cycle: perennial.

Size: eight inches to one foot tall.

This sweet-scented herb produces a pair of leaves (occasionally three) that extend above the flowers. Leaves are broadly ovate with smooth margins and parallel veins. Flowers have a waxy texture, they are bell-shaped with six petals and short stems, and they hang in loose, spiked clusters. The stalk is slender and often bends from the weight of the flowers. Berries are reddish orange, small and develop after the flowers have matured; they are inconspicuous and seldom seen. The rootstock is slender and produces a number of short, vertical, budding rootstocks that produce additional stalks.

Habitat: gardens, abandoned farms, shaded woods.

Poisonous parts: all parts.

Symptoms: handling can cause dermatitis. Ingesting causes irregular pulse, delirium, weakness, coma, death.

Medicinal uses: flower and rootstock tea for heart disease, fevers, diuretic, sedative; rootstock ointment for preventing scar tissue.

Notes: *Convallaria majalis* resembles the bulbs of wild leek. This favorite garden herb is as beautiful as it is deadly. The entire herb is extremely poisonous and ingesting the smallest amount is lethal; fatalities have occurred. Its fragrant sweet-smelling oil has been used to scent perfumes. From 1856 to 1968 it was used freely in medicine, but today its use can be practiced only under strict guidelines by a licensed practitioner. Medicinal use of this herb is strictly prohibited.

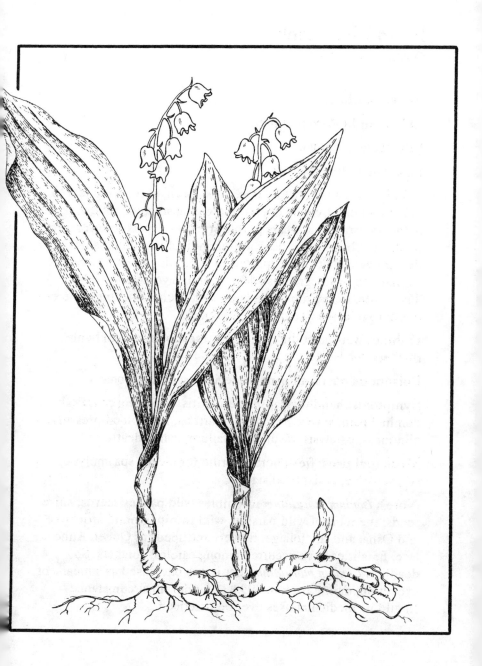

Poison Hemlock
Conium maculatum

Flowers: white.

In bloom: June–September.

Life cycle: biennial.

Size: two to five feet tall.

A foul-scented herb with large, dark green, parsleylike leaves that are finely divided and alternate on a smooth, hollow, branching stalk that bears purple streaks or spots. Flowers are small and cluster together forming individual, umbel-shaped flower heads that are supported by long, slender stems. Seeds are flat and ovate, greenish brown, and have notched edges. The white, fleshy taproot is large and often branching. The entire herb releases a foul scent if broken.

Habitat: wet-moist ditches, fields, meadows, stream banks, thickets, roadsides.

Poisonous parts: all parts; especially seeds, taproot.

Symptoms: handling causes dermatitis. Ingesting causes abdominal pain, severe headache, diarrhea, high blood pressure, blindness, paralysis, respiratory failure, coma, death.

Medicinal uses: fresh herb tincture for ulcers, spasmolytic, cancer, sedative, antiaphrodisiac.

Notes: *Conium maculatum* resembles wild parsley leaves; anise seeds; the roots of wild parsnip, wild turnip, ground artichoke and Osha; and the foliage, flowers and seeds of Queen Anne's lace. Fatalities have occurred among careless foragers. So deadly is *Conium maculatum* that it was once used as a means of execution, dating back to 399 B.C. Under no circumstance should its medicinal uses ever be practiced.

Pokeweed
Phytolacca americana

Flowers: white.

In bloom: July–September.

Berries: September–November.

Life cycle: perennial.

Size: five to ten feet tall.

This strong-scented herb has small upper leaves, and larger, lance-shaped, lower leaves with smooth, slightly wavy margins and prominent veins. Leaves alternate on a smooth, succulent, reddish stalk. Flowers are small and bloom in loose, elongated clusters. Berries are round, reddish black, and have a glossy shine. They form loose elongated clusters that often cause the stalk to bend from their weight. The taproot is large and fleshy.

Habitat: moist ground, fields, woodland edges, waste places.

Poisonous parts: all parts; especially berries, taproot.

Symptoms: handling can cause dermatitis. Ingesting causes painful burning in the mouth, cramps, nausea, vomiting, diarrhea, blurred vision, sweating, respiratory failure, convulsions, death.

Medicinal uses: leaves and taproot poultice for headaches, rheumatism, bruises, swellings, minor skin abrasions; taproot ointment for eczema, psoriasis; berry tea for arthritis, diarrhea; berry extract for hemorrhoids, cancer.

Notes: *Phytolacca americana* resembles asparagus shoots and horseradish root. Claimed to be extremely deadly, there are those who challenge its toxic nature. As a food, the leaves and green stalks (boiled twice) are said to make a good potherb, while the berries have been used for pie filling and for making jam. However, do not underestimate this herb's toxicity, incorrect preparation as well as a lethal overdose are probable, and fatalities have occurred. This herb is considered dangerous and its use is not recommended.

Red Baneberry
Actaea rubra

Flowers: white.

In bloom: May–June.

Berries: July–November.

Life cycle: perennial.

Size: two to three feet tall.

This small, attractive herb produces large, bright green, maplelike leaves that are lobed and have sharply toothed margins. Leaves are short-stemmed and divided into three's, they are supported by long, branching, alternating stems (lower stems clasping the stalk). The stalk is smooth and branching. Flowers bloom in tightly grouped clusters, their stamens are long and conspicuous, and extend well beyond the tiny petals. Berries are bright red (occasionally white) and have a waxy bloom, they develop in drooping clusters. The rootstock is thick and twisted, and begins just above the ground.

Habitat: moist woods, thickets, clearings, stream banks.

Poisonous parts: all parts; especially berries, rootstock.

Symptoms: stomach cramps, burning sensations, vomiting, headache, dizziness, delirium, rapid pulse, respiratory failure, death.

Medicinal uses: rootstock decoction for colds, coughs, menstrual irregularities; leaf poultice for sores, boils.

Notes: *Actaea rubra* resembles the leaves and berries of wild currant, and is considered extremely dangerous. As few as five berries contain enough poison to cause a lethal dose, and fatalities have occurred.

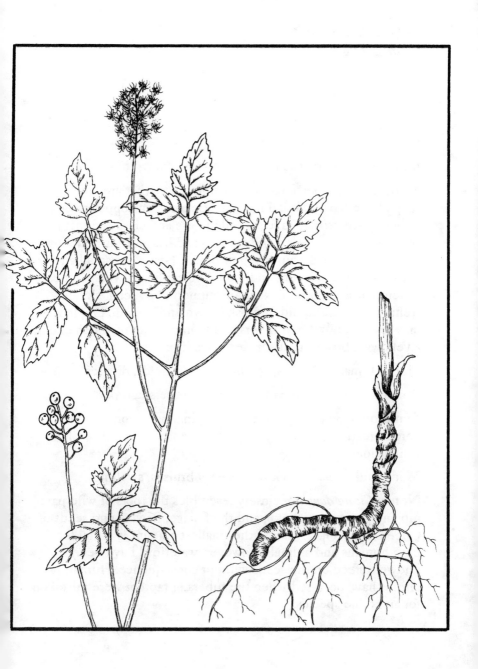

Western Water Hemlock
Cicuta douglasii

Flowers: white.

In bloom: June–September.

Life cycle: perennial.

Size: two to six feet tall.

A smooth, stout herb with compound leaves that are lance-shaped and have toothed margins. Leaves grow opposite on alternating stems that have a swollen base and clasp the main stalk. The stalk is thick and smooth and has a series of hollow chambers that make up its inner base. Flowers are small and cluster together forming individual flower heads which appear as semiflattened umbels that are supported by long, slender stems. Seeds are round, reddish brown and ribbed. The root may reveal a bundle of tubers or a taproot, both of which exude a yellowish brown, foul-scented juice if broken.

Habitat: marshes, bogs, streams, woods, fields, ditches.

Poisonous parts: all parts; especially tubers, taproot.

Symptoms: nausea, diarrhea, abdominal pain, vomiting, labored breathing, rapid-weak pulse, intense salivation, violent convulsions, death.

Medicinal uses: taproot poultice for bruises, swellings.

Notes: *Cicuta douglasii* closely resembles the roots of wild parsnip and ground artichoke; and the foliage, flowers and seeds of Queen Anne's lace. Eating the smallest amount is lethal for both humans and animals; however, waterfowl have been known to feed on the seeds without consequence. Human fatalities have occurred when the tubers or taproot were mistaken for an edible species.

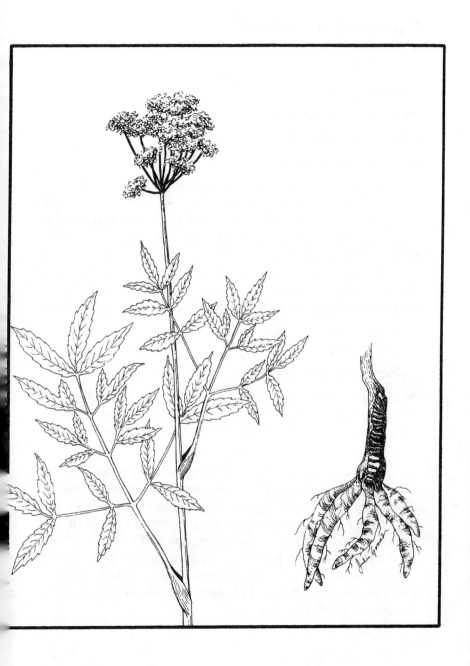

Creeping Buttercup
Ranunculus repens

Flowers: yellow.

In bloom: May–August.

Life cycle: perennial.

Size: two to three feet long.

This low and trailing herb has dark green leaves that are covered with short, stiff hairs that often reflect pale markings. Leaves are three-divided, toothed and have long, hairy stems that rise up from a creeping, hairy stalk. The stalk sends out runners that take root at the nodes. Flowers have five to seven overlapping petals, numerous stamens and hairy sepals, and are also supported by long, hairy stems. Seedpods are smooth, ovate and have a hooked beak. The rootstock is thick and fibrous.

Habitat: moist lawns, gardens, fields, pastures, roadsides, ditches, stream banks.

Poisonous parts: juices of fresh herb.

Symptoms: juices cause dermatitis. Ingesting the fresh herb causes severe burning blisters, stomachache, vomiting, diarrhea, paralysis of the nervous system, damage of the digestive system.

Notes: *Ranunculus repens* contains the same toxic properties as *Ranunculus acris*, except that its toxicity varies to some degree. However, both are poisonous only while the herb is fresh. Children have been poisoned after eating from the fresh herb, and livestock have also been poisoned. Goats and cows that graze on the fresh herb produce a tainted milk. As a food, the herb can be boiled several times until rendered safe, it can then be eaten like cooked greens. This herb is considered dangerous, and its use is not recommended.

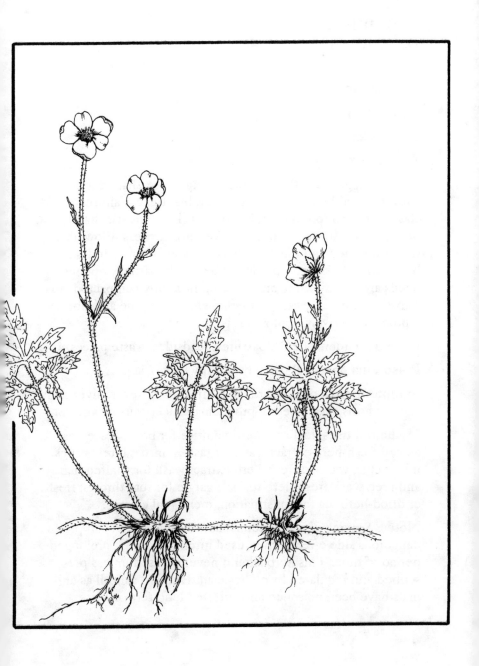

Groundsel
Senecio vulgaris

Flowers: yellow.

In bloom: year round.

Life cycle: annual.

Size: one to two feet tall.

A tall, straggly herb that produces long, lance-shaped leaves with rounded lobes and toothed margins. Leaves alternate and clasp a smooth (often branching) stalk. Lower leaves have fleshy stems, while the upper leaves are stemless. Flowers are short-stemmed and bloom in loose clusters from cylindrical bracts with darkened tips, and appear only partially opened. Seeds are downy white and develop in tightly compacted clusters; they are easily carried by the wind. The pale and fibrous taproot is relatively strong, but is easy to eradicate.

Habitat: gardens, fields, pastures, roadsides, waste places.

Poisonous parts: all parts; especially leaves, stalk.

Symptoms: loss of appetite, abdominal pain, severe liver damage, cirrhosis, suspected of producing cancer-causing agents.

Medicinal uses: leaf and stem poultice for boils, abscesses; cooled fresh-herb extract wash for rashes, insect bites, stings, minor cuts; warmed fresh-herb extract wash for chaffed hands and feet; weak fresh-herb tea as a gargle for sore throats; fresh or dried-herb tea for constipation, menstrual cramps.

Notes: *Senecio vulgaris* contains harmful toxins that can produce dangerous side effects when used internally over a prolonged period of time. This herb should never be used unless prescribed and regulated by a physician. Humans as well as animals have been poisoned and suffered long-term effects.

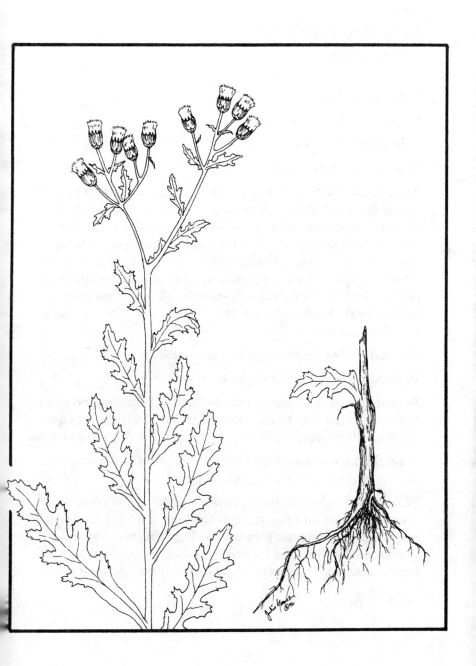

Meadow Buttercup
Ranunculus acris

Flowers: yellow.

In bloom: May–September.

Life cycle: perennial.

Size: two to three feet tall.

An attractive herb with dark green, stemless leaves that have five to seven divided, toothed segments. Leaves alternate on slender, hairy, branching stalks. Flowers can bloom solitary or in clusters from long, slender, hairy stems. Flowers produce five to seven overlapping petals that have a waxy texture and a glossy surface, and are supported by hairy sepals. Seedpods appear in clusters, they are small, smooth and have a prominent hooked beak. Each pod produces a single seed. The rootstock is a fibrous mass.

Habitat: fields, meadows, pastures, roadsides.

Poisonous parts: juices of the fresh herb.

Symptoms: juices cause severe dermatitis. Ingesting the fresh herb causes burning blisters, stomachache, vomiting, diarrhea, paralysis of the nervous system, damage of the digestive system.

Medicinal uses: leaf extract tincture for arthritis, rheumatism; taproot poultice for blisters, abscesses.

Notes: the juice of *Ranunculus acris* is highly irritating and can cause extensive internal damage. Cooking or drying expels its toxins which allows the greens to be used for food, and the dried seeds can be used for making baked goods. However, this herb is considered dangerous and its use is not recommended.

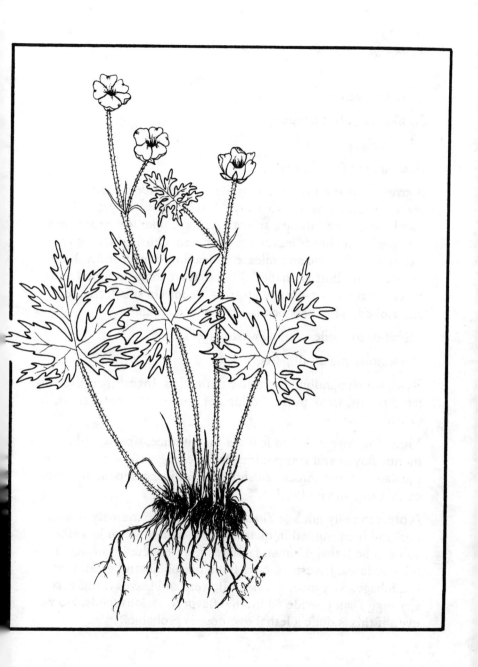

Tansy
Tanacetum vulgare

Flowers: yellow.

In bloom: July–October.

Life cycle: perennial.

Size: one to four feet tall.

A strong and stout herb that produces dark green, toothed leaves that are finely divided and fernlike. Leaves grow alternately on strong, fibrous, smooth stalks. Upper leaves are stemless, while the lower leaves are stemmed. Crushed leaves are extremely aromatic and release a pleasant lemony scent. Flowers are small, button-shaped disks that are long-stemmed and bloom in tight, flat-topped clusters. Seeds are small, slender and ribbed. The rootstock is shallow and creeping.

Habitat: roadsides, fields, waste places.

Poisonous parts: all parts.

Symptoms: handling can cause dermatitis. Ingesting causes dilated pupils, weak pulse, frothing of the mouth, convulsions, death.

Medicinal uses: chilled leaf tea for jaundice, worms, kidney ailments; flower and leaf poultice for swelling, inflammation; leaf inhalant for sore throats; fresh leaves for insect repellent; herb-extract tincture is abortive.

Notes: the oily juice of *Tanacetum vulgare* is extremely poisonous, and if consumed in quantity (one-half ounce or less) the result can be lethal. Human fatalities have resulted from accidental overdoses. Livestock have been poisoned after grazing on the foliage. As a food, the fresh flowers and leaves (used very sparingly) can provide additional flavor to various foods. However, if this is done a lethal overdose is probable.

Tomato
Lycopersicon esculentum

Flowers: yellow.

In bloom: June–August.

Berries: July–August.

Life cycle: annual.

Size: three to six feet tall.

This popular and well-known garden herb is covered with short, stiff hairs, and releases a strong, pleasant earthy scent. Its leaves are dark green and compounded with smaller leaflets interspersed among them. Leaves are short-stemmed, have lobed margins and alternate on a branching vinelike stalk. Flowers are small, delicate and bell-shaped, and nod toward the ground. Berries are red (occasionally yellow) and consist of a tender succulent pulp. They are generally three inches or less in diameter. The taproot is shallow and spreading.

Habitat: gardens.

Poisonous parts: all parts; except for berries.

Symptoms: handling can cause dermatitis. Ingesting causes nausea, abdominal pain, vomiting, constipation, diarrhea, weakness, labored breathing, trembling, numbness, paralysis, death.

Notes: *Lycopersicon esculentum* is extremely poisonous except for its berry (commonly called a vegetable). Widespread and radically cultivated in summer gardens, it's this herb's succulent berry that is so sought after. Fatalities have occurred among humans and livestock that dared to eat its other parts. People have died after drinking a tea made with the leaves and flowers. Livestock have died after grazing on the foliage. Historically, it was once believed that the berries were also poisonous, but today we know better.

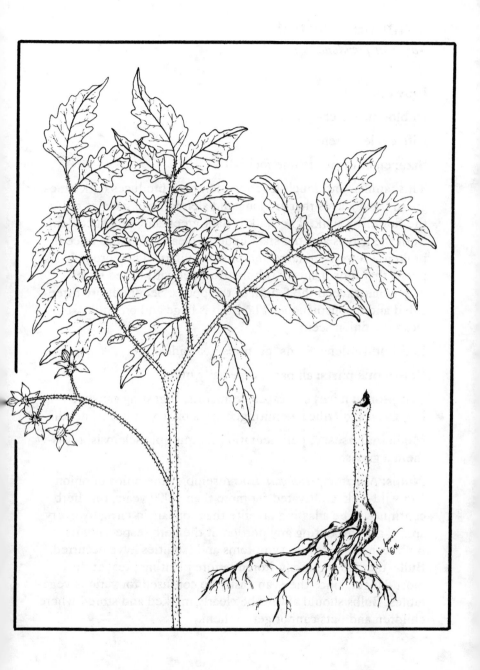

Trumpet Daffodil
Narcissus pseudonarcissus

Flowers: yellow.

In bloom: March–April.

Life cycle: perennial.

Size: eight inches to one foot tall.

This familiar and much-loved garden herb produces dark blue-green basal leaves that are long and slender, and grow as tall as the flowering stalk. The stalk is dark green and very succulent. Both the leaves and the stalk exude a clear, poisonous juice if broken. Flowers are large and bloom solitary. They produce six petals that form a showy tubular trumpet with frilled outer edges that exceed the length of the petals. Seedpods are three-sided and inconspicuous. The bulb is large and onionlike, but lacks the onion scent.

Habitat: gardens, fields, pastures, roadsides.

Poisonous parts: all parts; especially bulb.

Symptoms: juices can cause dermatitis. Ingesting causes sweating, nausea, diarrhea, vomiting, confusion, convulsions, death.

Medicinal uses: experimentation for multiple sclerosis, myasthemia gravis.

Notes: *Narcissus pseudonarcissus* resembles the bulbs of onion and wild leek. Cultivated for more than 1,000 years, this herb continues to be a lasting favorite that appears in virtually every spring garden. Eating any portion of the herb (especially its bulb) can cause severe symptoms and fatalities have occurred. Bulbs that are carelessly stored before planting present the most danger, since they can easily be confused for various vegetables. Bulbs should always be clearly marked and stored where children and pets cannot get to them.

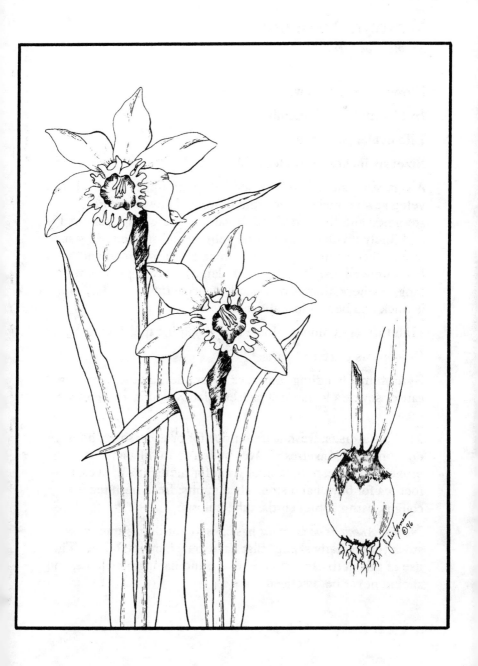

Western Anemone
Anemone occidentalis

Flowers: pale yellow.

In bloom: May–September.

Life cycle: perennial.

Size: six inches to two feet tall.

A very stout and densely haired herb with upper leaves that develop several inches below the flowers. They are short-stemmed and finely divided. Basal leaves are long-stemmed and finely divided. Flowers are solitary and supported by succulent stalks. Their showy petals are large, cup-shaped and have hairy undersides. Seed heads are large and conspicuous with long, feathery plumes that nearly conceal the stalk. The taproot is thick and begins just above the soil.

Habitat: rocky slopes, alpine and subalpine meadows.

Poisonous parts: all parts.

Symptoms: handling can cause severe dermatitis. Ingesting causes severe ulcerations, nausea, bloody vomiting, bloody diarrhea.

Medicinal uses: fresh leaf poultice for bruises, sores, boils, minor skin abrasions; fresh leaves boiled as an inhalant for colds, bronchial congestion; taproot wash for rheumatism, eyes; taproot tea for bowel and stomach ailments; fresh herb tea for coughs, asthma, bronchitis, tuberculosis.

Notes: *Anemone occidentalis* has caused poisoning among livestock (particularly sheep) that have grazed on its foliage. The use of this herb can produce severe and damaging results, and should never be practiced.

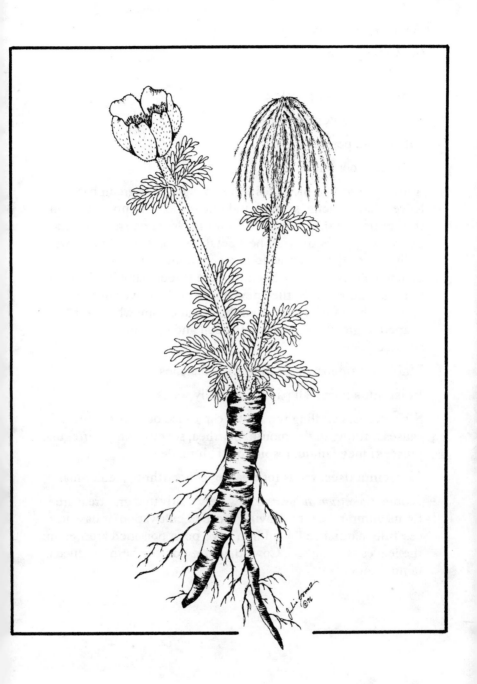

Autumn Crocus
Colchicum autumnale

Flowers: pink or purple.

In bloom: September–October.

Life cycle: perennial.

Size: one foot tall.

A lovely herb that produces three to eight dark green basal leaves that are long, smooth and linear. Leaves appear only in the spring and then die back. Flowers bloom on smooth, independent, leafless stalks. Their petals are long and slender with pointed tips that open wide to reveal numerous stamens with orange-colored anthers. Seedpods are three-chambered and contain numerous seeds; they develop with the leaves in the spring. The corm is large, dark brown and somewhat pear-shaped; it grows deep within the soil and contains a foul-scented juice.

Habitat: gardens, moist meadows, marshes.

Poisonous parts: all parts; especially seeds.

Symptoms: handling the leaves can cause dermatitis. Ingesting causes burning in the mouth, diarrhea, severe cramps, irregular pulse, kidney failure, respiratory failure, death.

Medicinal uses: seeds for treating gout, arthritis, leukemia.

Notes: *Colchicum autumnale* is widely cultivated and treasured for its autumn beauty. Having escaped cultivation, it has successfully naturalized. Children have been poisoned after eating the leaves and flowers. Cows that graze on the herb produce a tainted milk.

Foxglove
Digitalis purpurea

Flowers: pink, white or violet.

In bloom: June–August.

Life cycle: biennial.

Size: two to five feet tall.

This dazzling herb produces a rosette of large, velvety leaves in its first year, and the stalk and flowers in its second. Leaves are ovate to lance-shaped and have toothed margins. The lower leaves are large and basal, while the upper leaves are small and alternate on a slender, hairy, nonbranching stalk. Flowers are long and bell-shaped; they bloom in elongated clusters, generally from one side of the stalk, all pointing in the same direction. The stalk often bends from their weight. Inside each flower, and on the outer lips of the petals, are flecks of white and maroon. Seedpods are egg-shaped and have two-chambers that contain numerous seeds. The taproot is shallow and fibrous.

Habitat: gardens, fields, roadsides, woodland edges, burned ground.

Poisonous parts: all parts; especially leaves, seeds.

Symptoms: handling can cause dermatitis, nausea, headaches. Ingesting causes nausea, vomiting, severe headache, blurred vision, dizziness, bloody diarrhea, irregular pulse, hallucinations, convulsions, death.

Medicinal uses: second year leaves for heart ailments, blood pressure.

Notes: *Digitalis purpurea* is extremely dangerous and eating just two leaves is enough to cause fatal poisoning. Humans and livestock have died after eating the leaves or the flowers which contain the seeds. Having escaped cultivation, this herb successfully coexists in the wild where it often forms dense stands. Under no circumstance should its uses ever be practiced. Even in safe prescription form its dosage is nearly lethal.

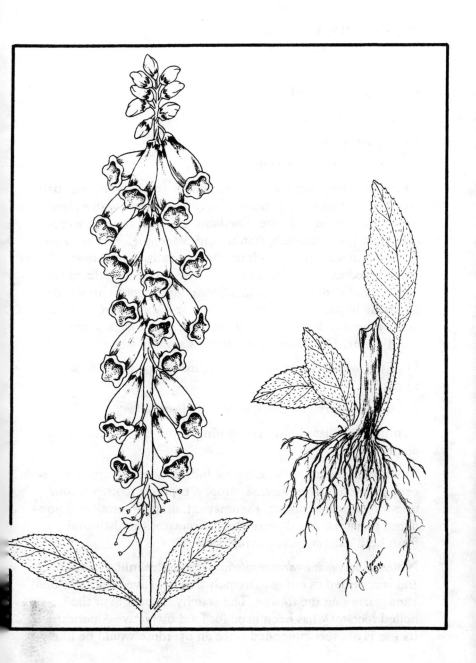

Spreading Dogbane
Apocynum androsaemifolium

Flowers: pink to red.

In bloom: May–August.

Life cycle: perennial.

Size: one to three feet tall.

This bushy herb has leaves that are dark green above, and pale green (sometimes hairy) below. Leaves are ovate with smooth margins, they are short-stemmed and grow opposite on a reddish stalk that is smooth, fibrous and branching. Flowers bloom in loose, drooping clusters from the leaf axils. They are small, bell-shaped and have long stems. Their petals are pale on the outside and dark on the inside. Seedpods are long and slender, and hang in pairs. When the pods dry and split open, they reveal numerous downy white seeds. The rootstock is smooth and slender. The entire herb contains a milky white juice.

Habitat: well-drained soil of fields, meadows, thickets, woods, roadsides.

Poisonous parts: all parts; especially leaves.

Symptoms: dilated pupils, vomiting, rapid pulse, heart failure, death.

Medicinal uses: rootstock tea for indigestion, constipation, fevers, gallstones, liver disease, dropsy, syphilis; rootstock tincture for nausea, vomiting, rheumatism, dropsy, vermifuge; powdered rootstock as a diuretic; boiled rootstock for hair tonic; fresh herb extract for removing warts.

Notes: *Apocynum androsaemifolium* resembles milkweed shoots and is regarded as being extremely deadly. Livestock have died after grazing on the foliage. The starchy inner core of the boiled rootstock has been used for food by Native Americans. Its use is not recommended since an overdose would be likely.

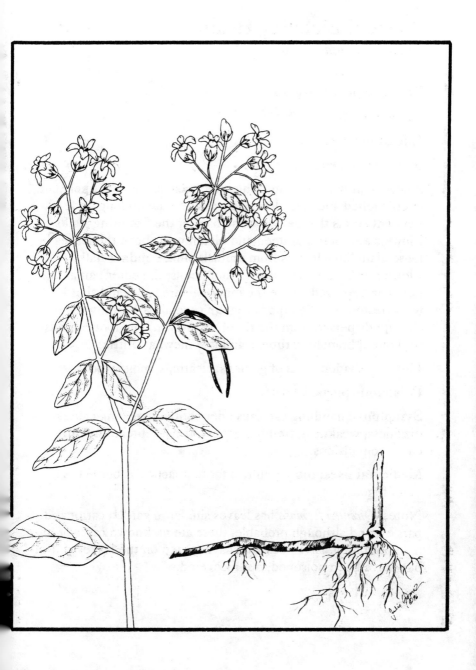

Western Bleeding Heart
Dicentra formosa

Flowers: pink or white.

In bloom: March–July.

Life cycle: perennial.

Size: one to two feet tall.

A succulent herb with soft blue-green leaves that are finely cut, deeply lobed and carrotlike. Leaves alternate on long, independent stems that gather at the base of the flowering stalks. Flowers are short-stemmed and bloom well above the leaves in loose, dangling clusters from reddish pink, bending stalks. Flowers are heart-shaped with four petals; the outer pair are inflated and spurred, while the inner pair are small and slender with crested tips. Seedpods contain several dark, shiny seeds that are dispersed from the tip of the flower. The root consists of slender, branching tubers, and is somewhat brittle.

Habitat: shaded areas of gardens, clearings, moist woods.

Poisonous parts: all parts.

Symptoms: handling can cause dermatitis. Ingesting causes dizziness, weakness, trembling, nervousness, breathing difficulty, convulsions.

Medicinal uses: tuber poultice for toothaches; tuber tea as a vermifuge.

Notes: *Dicentra formosa* has leaves similar to garden carrot and parsley, and although probable, there are no known cases of human poisoning. Livestock that have grazed on the leaves and tubers have been poisoned, but recovered.

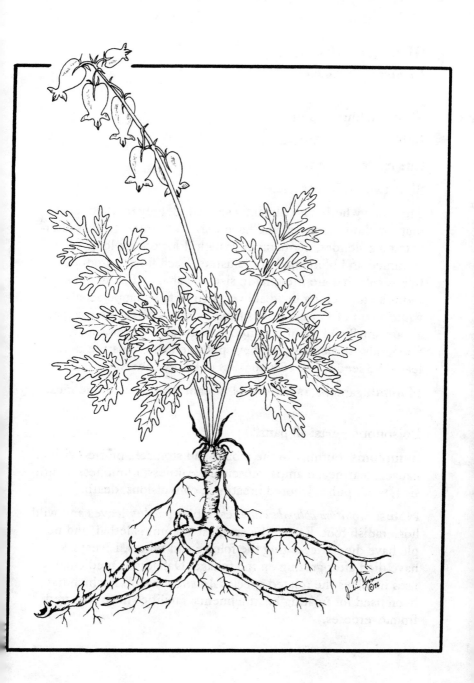

Blue Monkshood
Aconitum columbianum

Flowers: blue or purple.

In bloom: June–August.

Life cycle: perennial.

Size: two to six feet tall.

This showy herb has palmately shaped, deeply toothed leaves that are short-stemmed and have a sticky texture. Leaves alternate on a slender, nonbranching stalk. Flowers are long-stemmed and bloom in loose clusters. Each flower produces five sepals that are irregular in size and shape. The upper sepal forms a tall, arching hood above a pair of fan-shaped sepals, while a pair of slender sepals hang below. The two to five petals are small and rounded, and are concealed by the sepals. Seedpods are slender and they split open when mature to release the seeds. The root consists of fleshy tubers.

Habitat: gardens, moist woods, stream banks, subalpine meadows.

Poisonous parts: all parts.

Symptoms: burning in the mouth and stomach, blurred vision, nausea, diarrhea, cramps, muscular weakness, numbness, confusion, weak pulse, labored breathing, convulsions, death.

Notes: *Aconitum columbianum* resembles parsley leaves and wild horseradish root. Eating the smallest amount is lethal, and people have died after eating the foliage and tubers. Livestock have died after grazing on the foliage. Dangerous medicinal uses involves the related species *Aconitum napellus*, which has been used for treating heart ailments; fatalities have occurred from overdoses.

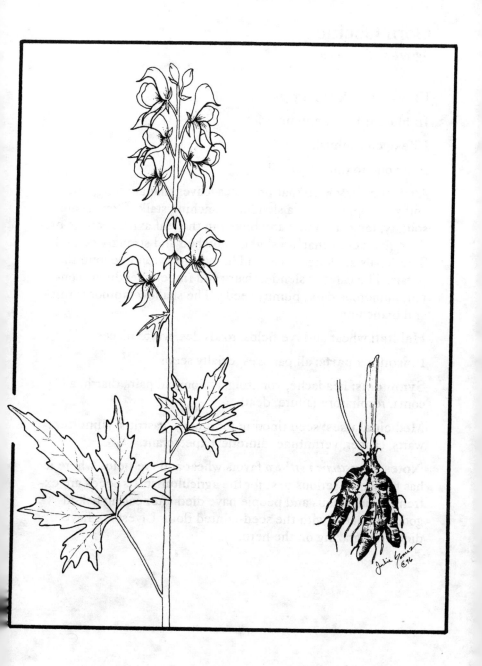

51

Corn Cockle
Agrostemma githago

Flowers: pink to purple.

In bloom: July–September.

Life cycle: annual.

Size: one to three feet tall.

A tall and silky herb that produces leaves that are long, linear and grow opposite on a slender, branching stalk. Flowers are solitary, long-stemmed and bloom in the leaf axils. Flowers produce five petals that are slightly notched and strongly veined. The sepals are long, linear and hairy, and extend beyond the petals. The calyx is slender, hairy and ribbed. Seedpods contain numerous dark, bumpy seeds. The shallow taproot is thick and branching.

Habitat: wheat and rye fields, roadsides, waste places.

Poisonous parts: all parts; especially seeds.

Symptoms: headache, vomiting, abdominal pain, diarrhea, coma, respiratory failure, death.

Medicinal uses: seed tincture for dropsy, gastritis, jaundice, warts, cancer, vermifuge, diuretic, expectorant.

Notes: *Agrostemma githago* favors wheat and rye fields where it has become a serious pest for the agriculturist. Its seeds are extremely poisonous and people have died after eating baked goods prepared with the seed-tainted flour. Livestock have died after grazing on the herb.

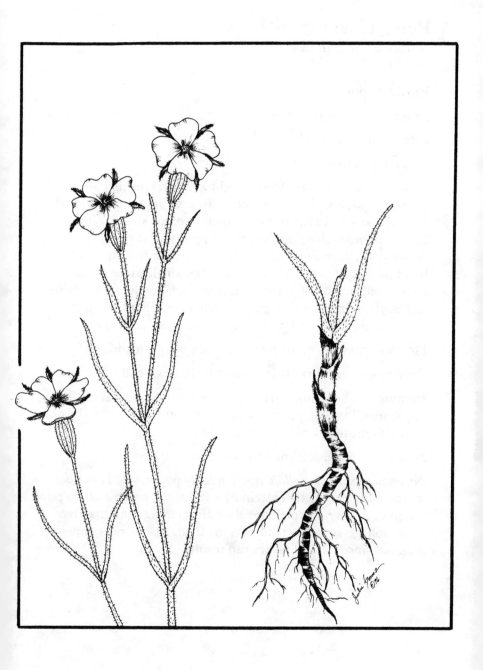

Poison Larkspur
Delphinium trolliifolium

Flowers: purple.

In bloom: April–June.

Life cycle: perennial.

Size: two to five feet tall.

A tall, robust herb with large, bright-green leaves that are deeply divided with pointed lobes. Leaves are long-stemmed, slightly hairy and alternate on smooth, hollow stalks. Flowers bloom in loose, elongated clusters on individual stems. Each flower consists of five sepals that are irregular in shape and bend backward to reveal the petals (two small white petals above, and two small purple petals below). Seedpods are ovate and contain dark, flattened seeds that are released when the pods mature. The rootstock is thick and woody.

Habitat: gardens, moist woods, stream banks, roadsides.

Poisonous parts: all parts; especially leaves, seeds.

Symptoms: handling can cause dermatitis, tingling sensations, numbness. Ingesting causes nausea, vomiting, abdominal pain, convulsions, respiratory failure, death.

Medicinal uses: seed tincture for head and body lice.

Notes: *Delphinium trolliifolium* is deadly poisonous. Livestock (particularly cattle) are extremely vulnerable, and many are poisoned each year. People have died after eating the attractive green foliage as salad greens. Its medicinal use is not recommended since painful rashes can result.

Woody Nightshade
Solanum dulcamara

Flowers: violet (occasionally white).

In bloom: May–September.

Berries: September–November.

Life cycle: perennial.

Size: one to eight feet long.

A persistent, strong, vinelike herb that produces a foul scent. Leaves are long-stemmed with smooth margins, and may or may not be hairy. Leaf shapes vary, some are ovate, while others produce a lobed base. Small, modified leaves develop in the leaf axils. Leaves alternate on a slender, tough, woody stalk. Flowers bloom in loose, branching clusters. They are star-shaped and produce five pointed petals that curve backward to reveal a slender yellow cone that contains five stamens. Berries are bright red, ovate and appear in drooping clusters. The rootstock is slender, woody and fibrous.

Habitat: roadsides, waste places, thickets, open woods.

Poisonous parts: all parts; especially berries.

Symptoms: abdominal pain, vomiting, weak pulse, convulsions, paralysis, death.

Medicinal uses: fresh leaves and stalks for various skin disorders, warts, tumors, gout, rheumatism, bronchitis, promotes sweating, diuretic.

Notes: *Solanum dulcamara* is poisonous to humans, livestock and domestic animals. If eaten in quantity, the results can be fatal. As few as ten berries are enough to cause fatal poisoning in children. Birds (such as the song sparrow) are not affected after consuming the berries. This herb is persistent once it becomes established.

Cocklebur
Xanthium strumarium

Flowers: green.

In bloom: July–November.

Life cycle: annual.

Size: one to two feet tall.

A scraggly herb with broad ovate-shaped leaves that are un-evenly lobed, have toothed margins, and are long-stemmed. Leaves have a rough texture and alternate on smooth, branching stalks. Flowers are small and inconspicuous, and bloom from the leaf axils. Seedpods are hard and woody, and covered with short, recurved barbs. On the ends of each pod is a pair of conspicuous horns. Each pod contains a pair of irregular-shaped seeds. The taproot is long and woody.

Habitat: fields, thickets, stream banks, roadsides, waste places.

Poisonous parts: all parts; especially seeds.

Symptoms: handling can cause dermatitis. Ingesting causes nausea, loss of appetite, depression, convulsions, death.

Medicinal uses: leaf tea for rheumatism, cystitis, tuberculosis, kidney disease, diuretic; boiled seedpods for diarrhea; seed tincture is antiseptic; taproot for scrofulous tumors.

Notes: *Xanthium strumarium* is poisonous to both humans and livestock. Although probable, there are no reports of human fatalities, but livestock have died after eating the tender young shoots and spiny seedpods. This herb is extremely dangerous and prolonged or misuse can result in a lethal overdose.

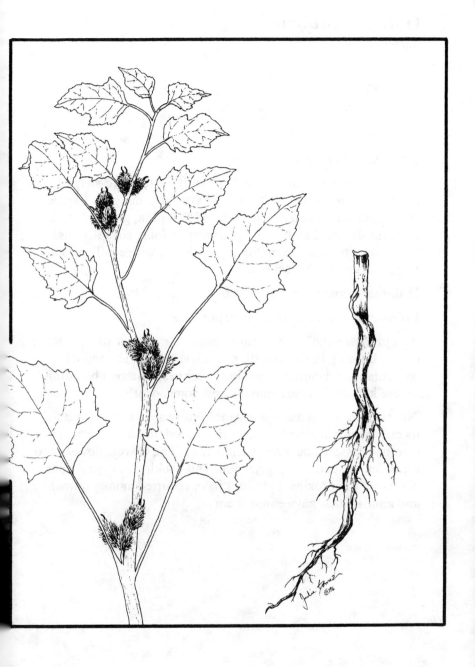

Garden Rhubarb
Rheum rhaponticum

Flowers: green.

In bloom: June–July.

Life cycle: perennial.

Size: three to four feet tall.

A very large and stout garden herb with broad ovate-shaped leaves that are heavily veined and have wavy margins. Leaves are supported by long, succulent, reddish pink, grooved stalks. Flowers are small and bloom profusely in long, conspicuous, branching clusters. Seedpods are small and winged. The root-stock consists of thick tubers.

Habitat: gardens, old farm sites.

Poisonous parts: all parts; except stalks.

Symptoms: handling the leaves can cause dermatitis. Ingesting causes burning in the mouth, nausea, vomiting, abdominal pain, diarrhea, labored breathing, weakness, internal bleeding, severe kidney damage, convulsions, coma, death.

Notes: *Rheum rhaponticum* is widely cultivated and desired for its tart-tasting leaf stalks that make up a delicious variety of summer desserts, beverages and wines. The leaves, flowers and rootstock are extremely poisonous and cooking or drying does not expel their toxins. Fatalities have occurred among humans and animals that have eaten them.

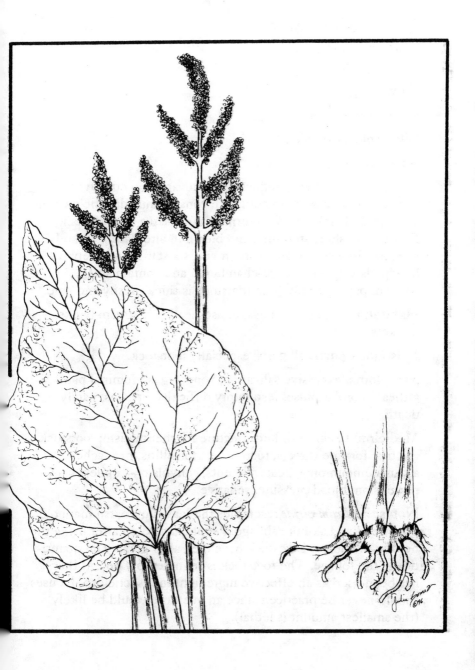

Green Hellebore
Veratrum viride

Flowers: green.

In bloom: April–July.

Life cycle: perennial.

Size: two to eight feet tall.

This tall, bushy herb produces large, ovate-shaped leaves. Above, the leaves are smooth with conspicuous ribs, below they are slightly hairy. Leaves alternate and clasp a smooth stalk. Flowers are short-stemmed and bloom in alternating spiked clusters. Flowers are small and reveal six star-shaped sepals. Seedpods are ovate, three-chambered and contain small, winged, papery seeds. The rootstock is thick, fleshy and pale.

Habitat: mountainous areas, moist meadows, stream banks, thickets.

Poisonous parts: all parts; especially rootstock.

Symptoms: excessive salivation, vomiting, abdominal pain, diarrhea, irregular pulse, respiratory difficulty, spasms, paralysis, death.

Medicinal uses: fresh herb tincture for rheumatism; rootstock tincture for sore throats, toothaches, tonsillitis, headaches, asthma, pneumonia, heart ailments, convulsions, epilepsy, hypertension, blood pressure, sedative.

Notes: *Veratrum viride* resembles the leaves of marsh marigold, pokeweed and skunk cabbage. People have died after using the herb in medicine. Livestock have died after grazing on quantities of the foliage. The rootstock is so incredibly potent that it has been used as an effective ingredient in insecticides. Its uses should never be practiced since an overdose would be likely (the smallest amount is lethal).

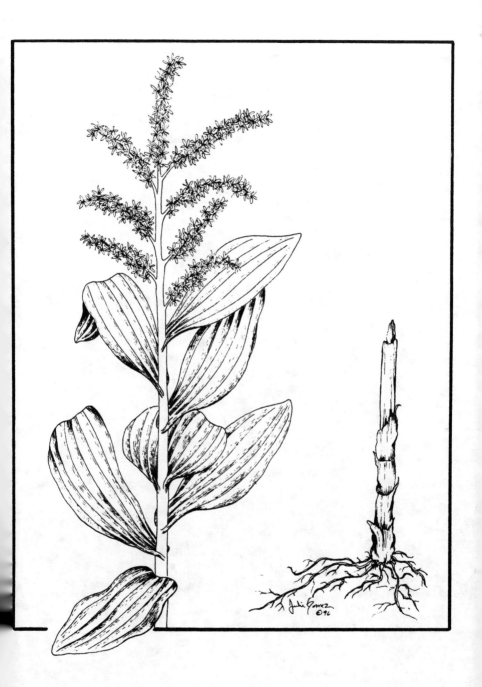